Boyhood in England

CHAPTER 1

Wilfred silently cursed his older brother as he crept over the beach. "Can you imagine," Wilfred thought aloud, "returning home without even seeing a duck?" His older brother, Al, was a real sissy for sure!

The beaches around Parkgate were all sand, and birds abounded both there and in the neighbouring marshes. There were ducks, sandpipers, oyster diggers, divers, waders, gulls, terns, and the occasional geese which flew over the marshes in great V-shaped formations. Hunting was great fun for a thirteen-year-old boy living in England in 1878.

That day had not been a good one for hunting. The marshes were wet and cold and the beach was damp. It was still too early in the year for good hunting. Al and Wilfred had not shot a single bird and were tired from walking down the long beach.

"What sense does it make, Wilfred? Even if we shoot a stupid bird we have no dog to go into the water to retrieve it," Al had concluded and then marched off home.

Wilfred knew that he would solve that problem when he came to it. The darkness of evening was quickly approaching as he turned and looked back up the beach in the direction his brother had gone. Instead of following Al, he stayed at the beach, determined to find some birds. As he rounded a small cove, he heard the faint cry of a curlew. The bird was still distant but its call carried clearly over the still waters of the evening.

Wilfred stopped in his tracks and listened. His eyes scanned the sky and his ears strained for sounds along the shore. He heard the water breaking gently on the beach, the sand hissing, the occasional tasteless gull calling; and then again he heard it, this time more closely. It was definitely a curlew coming to the shore to rest for the night. He dropped to one knee in the wet sand, aimed the gun out across the harbour and waited for the bird to call again or appear. Lucky for him, he thought, that it was still light enough to see.

The young Wilfred Grenfell, described by Pierre Berton as "the Lawrence of Arabia type"

One of Wilfred's ancestors, Sir Richard Grenville

Then the bird appeared, close overhead. She winged a few quick strokes and then glided down closer to the beach. Wilfred waited till she finished one of her glides and then fired. The bird tumbled over and fell. He watched carefully where she hit the water and then he tore off his shirt and pants. He splashed out into the chilly sea water without a thought for the cold. He ran till the water reached to his knees and waist, and then swam a few strokes before he reached the bird. Lobbing it back over his head in the manner of a water polo player he guided his catch back to shore.

Hardly had he regained the sand when he heard the cry again and again. Other curlews were flying in towards shore through the gathering dusk. Finding his gun, he slid another shell into the chamber and fired. He looked up and saw two curlews tumble out of the sky and behind them a whole flock was flying towards the shore, mindless of his firing. He fired again and again, ignoring the sharp pain in his shoulder from the big gun's recoil. When he feared that the tide would carry off his prizes he leaped again into the water and swam out after the fallen birds. Treading water, he tossed them all in to the shore and returned, jubilant.

There was not a happier boy than Wilfred Grenfell in all of Cheshire that evening. He stood shivering on the cold beach to survey his catch of curlews. Shaking himself dry as best he could, he jumped back into his clothes and tied the birds together with a length of cord which he swung over his shoulder. Then he started off in the direction of the Big House, Mostyn House school for boys which was owned and run by his father.

The Reverend A.S. Grenfell was Wilfred's father and through him Wilfred was related to a distinguished line of English heroes. Tennyson's famous poem, *Revenge,* tells of the exploits of one of them, Sir Richard Grenville, who cried, "Fight on! Fight on!" to his men even though his ship was almost destroyed by the enemy. Another ancestor was John Grenville who fought in England's defense against the invasion by the Spanish Armada and who boarded the ship of the Spanish Admiral with his sword in his hand. Basil Grenville was the commander of the army of Cornwall who fought for King Charles and was killed in 1643. All were related to Wilfred on his father's side of the family. All were brave fighting men

who fought hard and even died for what they believed was right.

Wilfred with his mother

On his mother's side of the family the Hutchinsons' tradition was similar. His mother's father was a colonel in the Royal Engineers of India. Four of her brothers were colonels or generals of the British overseas force in India. Her eldest brother, Wilfred's uncle, fought in the Indian mutiny and played a prominent part in the famous defence of Lucknow. Another uncle was killed in a war on the Northwest Frontier of India.

It was the fighting tradition on his father's side of the family that now troubled Wilfred as he made his way home. He could imagine his father's angry words and could feel the sting of a few stiff cuffs around the ears for his staying out so late.

His previous joy turned to gloom as he walked in the darkness along the damp sand with the string of birds hanging like so many albatrosses around his neck. When he did reach the Big House, as the villagers called the school, it was after nine o'clock. His mother and father and the Welsh matron who took care of the house in their absence were up waiting for him.

"Where were you, boy?" asked the Reverend Algernon Grenfell with the anger rising in his voice.

"Shooting curlew, sir. Look, I shot twenty."

"But you're wet," his mother cried.

"I had to swim out and retrieve the birds," he explained.

Wilfred's mother gasped.

"Swum out and got the birds, did you?" asked his father, suddenly softening his tone.

"Took off my clothes first, sir; laid them on the sand so I wouldn't get them wet."

"Good boy, that's how it's done. I remember when I was a lad we were shooting ducks one day. . ."

"Really, Algernon," Mrs. Grenfell spoke in exasperation. "Go to your room, Wilfred, and get out of those wet clothes."

Father looked somewhat embarrassed and Matron took the string of curlews from Wilfred's neck. He went up to his room and got into bed. His brother Al and his younger brother Cecil came into the room and asked him to tell them about his adventure, but he would not give them the satisfaction of hearing his story. He would only show them the black and blue bruise on his right shoulder from the recoils of the gun. Later as he lay alone in his bed, he thought about his day and considered it a qualified success.

The Sands of Dee CHAPTER 2

In later life Wilfred was to boast that every inch of the
Sands of Dee was dear to him. The old river Dee ran out
into the sea at Parkgate and carried with it tons of sand
from the interior of the island. Nearly twenty kilometres
inland was the ancient city of Chester, famous even in
the time of the Romans. Ships had sailed up to Chester
and this made it an important shipping port. Sand had
gradually clogged up the river, and by Wilfred's time no
ships could navigate the shallow Dee.

Wilfred hiked and hunted birds along the shores of
the Dee and collected specimens of various birds and
insects for his own study. He became quite an expert at
stuffing and mounting birds and his brother Al helped
by building little display cases.

Al may have been a sissy but he was no coward. This
was revealed to Wilfred one night when their parents
were on summer vacation and the school was empty.
The brothers were left in the hands of the Welsh matron
whose difficult task it was to keep them from mischief. It
was Al who decided upon a robbery to liven up their
summer. He explained the plan to Wilfred and the two of
them carried it out one night when the unsuspecting
matron was asleep.

*The Grenfell brothers:
Cecil, Algernon, and Wilfred in
1907*

They crept out through their windows and ran around to the storeroom where all the school provisions were kept. Like professionals, they glued brown paper to the window glass and then cut out the putty around it with a knife. They removed the glass to gain entry to the building. They stole biscuits, sweets, and a bottle of wine, which they consumed before dawn and then sneaked back to their rooms. Wilfred found the adventure so exciting that he retold it in his autobiography forty years later.

At thirteen years of age Wilfred showed no early signs that he would one day become a famous missionary. Both he and his brother were reluctant church goers. The sexton once reported to their father that they were writing chalk marks on the pew in front of them. Another time they were caught cooking chocolate on the church's steam pipes during the sermon. Both were duly punished for these crimes. Like his ancestors, young Grenfell was more interested in adventurous pursuits such as shooting, sailing, swimming, boxing and horse-back riding.

His abilities as an athlete stood him in good stead when he entered Marlborough boy's school at the age of fourteen. Although he was young and alone among six hundred other boys, he was always able to take care of himself. Once when he was pushed around by a bully, Wilfred fought back and gave the fellow a good beating with his bare knuckles. He became well respected by his fellow students and after a number of fights in which he emerged as winner he was nicknamed The Beast because of his thick hair and his readiness to fight.

To the victor went the spoils, and it was as a result of one of his fights at Marlborough that Wilfred managed to get a bed near the window in his dormitory. Through this window he would often escape, long after the doors of the dormitory had been closed for the night.

At Marlborough Wilfred met a fellow student called Mad G. who was befriended by no one, and was forced to keep very much to himself. The reason why the boys treated Mad G. in this manner was that he did not like the same things as they did. He was a brilliant student who would sit at the foot of Wilfred's bed and explain

A bicycle excursion in France This was a group of Grenfell relatives. Wilfred is second from the far right, and his brother Cecil is third.

his schemes for developing a self-steering torpedo or an airplane. He was a genius at mathematics and chemistry but he had been spoiled at home by his parents and five sisters. He had no brothers, and Marlborough was his introduction into a rough and tumble world where he was not the centre of attention. The thing about Mad G. which really turned the other boys against him was that he had no interest in sports and athletic competition which were the backbone of the school program.

One day as Wilfred and Mad G. left the classroom some of the boys threw a lump of coal which struck the unfortunate Mad G. in the head. The injury caused the loss of a great amount of blood. Grenfell took him to surgery where the old Doctor Fungi patched up the wound which was more bloody than it was serious. Wilfred was shocked that a group of boys would gang up on so defenceless a fellow as Mad G., and he decided that the matter needed rectifying. He carefully avoided Mad G's enemies when they were in great numbers, but when he found them singly or in pairs he waded into them and made the fur fly. Mad G. was never again bothered while he was in Wilfred's company.

Another character whom Wilfred met at Marlborough and who made a lasting impression on him was Doctor Fungi. The old doctor's real name was Fergus but he was nicknamed Fungi by the malicious boys at the school. Often if the boys were late for chapel, or if they wanted to avoid it all together, they would fake some illness and the kindly old doctor usually obliged by excusing them.

In later years Wilfred remembered some of the tricks he and other boys used. One way to get a "sick cut" from Doctor Fungi was to trip, fall down and get a bloody nose. Another way was by coughing. Doctor Fungi had a barrel of cough medicine, which was his own concoction, and if a boy were willing to drink the vile mixture, he would pretend to have a bad cough.

A little soap in the eyes gave all the symptoms of eye strain and was a frequent trick used by the boys. What impressed Wilfred about Fungi was not his gullibility so much as his concern for the boys in his charge. This was not a common characteristic of many of the masters at Marlborough or at the other schools of that day.

The Young Intern CHAPTER 3

Wilfred had finished his school training by 1883 and in that year his father called him home. After the usual welcome by the other members of the family, he and his father sat alone in the family study. Wilfred noted the little cases he and Al had made to display their mounted sea birds. Each bird perched on a shelf or on a table, stopped in time at the exact moment of its capture, and Wilfred could relive a dozen boyish adventures as he looked around the room. He noticed that his father looked a lot older than he ever remembered seeing him.

"Son, I'm going to give up the boys' school and become a full time clergyman. The strain of doing both is beginning to catch up with me."

"That is quite a surprise, sir. Will you be selling the Big House?"

"No. I plan to lease it for seven years until your brother Algernon is ready to take it over."

"I know that he often told me he would like to follow in your footsteps."

"What about you, Wilfred? What do you intend to do with your life now that you are finished public school?"

"I was thinking about becoming a doctor, sir."

"A doctor? It's an admirable profession no doubt, but none of the Grenfells were ever doctors."

"None of the Grenfells were ever ministers, sir, before you became one."

His father paused thoughtfully and then smiled at this remark. "Yes, that's true. That's true. I always liked to swim against the tide." His father chuckled to himself. "I'll tell you what I'll do. I have just been accepted as a chaplain at the London Hospital. If you want to come to London with me I'll pay for your studies at the hospital's medical school." Wilfred beamed his approval and the arrangements were soon made.

When he came to London he found the squalor and filth of the London slums around the hospital quite a contrast to the beautiful Sands of Dee. London Hospital was the largest hospital in the whole of the British Isles. Its huge wards contained almost a thousand beds. This

As a youth Grenfell was courageous and daring. His daring shows in a different way on this photo — bold, striped socks.

In the centre of the photo are Dr. Treves and Wilfred, with a group of boys from a boys' camp in 1891, the year before he went to Newfoundland for the first time.

was before the days of modern medicine, long before penicillin or even aspirin were discovered. Doctors knew little about infection and bacteria, and sterile operating rooms were still a thing of the future. Surgeons at London Hospital usually operated in their oldest and dirtiest clothes because operations were very messy. Often they were done without the aid of an anesthetic.

Equally bad was the medical school. There was little discipline, and students frequently did not attend their classes. When they did attend, they were continually playing pranks and annoying their teachers. Wilfred was surprised at one of his first classes in botany when a student poured a solution of foul smelling carbon bisulfide all over the professor's platform. He was no longer surprised at such pranks when at a later class someone released several live pigeons which had been meant for study. The whole class immediately opened fire on them with pea-shooters. Even Wilfred was caught up in this lax attitude towards his studies. He recorded in his autobiography that he attended few classes and often bribed a fellow student to mark him present.

The robust Grenfell did not neglect his athletic interests while he was at medical school. He continued to box, sail and exercise, and was a member of the hospital teams in cricket, football and rowing. He won inter-hospital trophies for football twice, and would have been welcomed to play on the united hospitals' team except that he did not enjoy their social life of drinking and carousing. He was also a champion hammer thrower and would practise alone for hours in Victoria Park. During one term he was in residence at Oxford University and easily made their excellent soccer team.

There were several men at the London Hospital who made a lasting impression on the young Grenfell, and the most important of these was his professor of surgery, Sir Frederick Treves. After Joseph Lister publicized the necessity of sterile operating rooms, hospitals rushed to install boilers which filled the operating rooms with carbolic steam to kill germs. Treves was the first to discard this innovation and replace it with a thorough scrubbing of the surgeon's hands and the use of clean gowns.

At about the same time, rubber gloves were being used for the first time in surgery in Johns Hopkins Hospital in Baltimore, Maryland. There was also an important discovery being made at this time by a German physician, Robert Koch. What was the discovery he made?

He often told his students, "Gentlemen, the secret of surgery is the nailbrush." Treves also taught his students the great importance of being self-reliant. He felt that a doctor can win his patient's confidence only if he is specific and definite in his diagnosis, and takes upon himself full responsibility for the patient's treatment. Once Treves was working with a student who had diagnosed a patient's injured leg by concluding: "It might be a fracture, sir, or it might only be sprained."

Treves replied, "The patient is not interested to know that it *might* be measles or it *might* be a toothache. The patient wants to know what is the matter, and it is your business to tell him, or he will go to a quack who will inform him at once." Treves went on to become Royal Physician to King Edward VII.

Years later in Labrador when Grenfell was the only doctor for miles along the coast, this self-reliance helped him to diagnose difficult cases confidently. It was through the advice of his teacher Sir Frederick Treves that Grenfell eventually found his way to Labrador and began his missionary work there.

The biggest influence upon Grenfell's life during the final years of his training in London Hospital did not come from the hospital at all. It had, in fact, nothing to

The Rev. Dwight L. Moody Moody was an American revivalist who became established with the help of Ira D. Sankey, a famous evangelistic singer of the time.

do with medicine, but rather it had to do with religion. Up to this point in his life Grenfell could not have been considered particularly religious. His upbringing had instilled in him a disdain for carousing, and his instinctive good will towards the unfortunate can be seen in his attitude towards people like Mad G.

Grenfell's religious feeling was aroused one evening when he was returning from a sick call in the Shadwell district of London. As he walked he saw a large tent which had been erected to house an evangelical meeting. He stepped in to see what it was all about. This was in 1885, and he was twenty years old. As the young medical student entered the tent a long, boring prayer was in progress, so he stayed long enough to satisfy his curiosity.

He later wrote, "Suddenly the leader, whom I learned afterwards was D.L. Moody, called out to the audience." Grenfell was immediately impressed by the man and stayed to listen to what he had to say. Moody challenged his audience to live their lives as Christ would if he were in their place.

What impressed Grenfell was that the people with Moody were very religious, but they were also natural athletes — men like the Studd brothers. Grenfell decided Moody was worth listening to, and he attended the rest of his lectures. By the end of the lecture series, Grenfell felt called to preach the word of God to the poor, and he began immediately.

He went into taverns and persuaded sailors to sign a pledge to give up drinking alcohol. He often risked his safety because he was sometimes attacked by drunks or forced into fights by irate tavern-keepers whose business he was ruining. He relished a good fist fight because he usually won. He worked in his spare time and on weekends setting up flophouses for the poor and homeless. These places often became the last refuge of alcoholics, who begged or occasionally stole from Grenfell and his helpers. The drunkards whom they helped considered Grenfell and his men to be "harmless and gullible imbeciles". Nevertheless, many of the men benefited from Grenfell's concern.

D.L. Moody had far-reaching effects during the time he spent in England. With funds collected as donations, and from profits from the sale of Gospel Hymns, *a work by Moody and Sankey, Moody established Northfield Seminary for Girls, Mt. Hermon School for Boys, Farwell Hall and the School for Bible Study at Northfield.*

Grenfell went on to establish schools for boys from the slums. His difficulties and frustrations are almost humorous to read today, nearly one hundred years later, but they must have tested the character of a young man barely twenty-one years old. Grenfell's next project was to organize summer camps for the boys. There he won their respect as a boxer, if not for the spiritual advice he offered them.

Grenfell believed that serving God was connected to helping people, and this concept is important in understanding the man and his life's work.

A scene from the London docks in Grenfell's time

CHAPTER 4 **The Fisherman's Doctor**

When Wilfred graduated as a qualified doctor in 1886, Sir Frederick Treves suggested that he join the medical mission to the deep sea fishermen who worked around the coast of England. Grenfell did just this, and for several years the young doctor sailed around the coast and treated injured fishermen who were often at sea for months at a time. Besides healing, he often conducted religious services and tried to persuade the men to stop wasting their wages on alcohol when they arrived in port.

Grenfell soon won the confidence of those adventurous, hard-working men, for they recognized in the young doctor something of the zest for life which was their own. Grenfell saw in them the adventurous seafaring spirit of his ancestors, Richard and John Grenville. He enjoyed working with them not because of

Grenfell's staff for the Mission to Deep Sea Fishermen, 1889

Grenfell is in the second row, third from the left.

the self-sacrifice which it demanded, but because the work suited his stalwart nature. He soon came to appreciate the many problems facing these men and he set to work to remedy as many of them as he could.

One problem was loneliness. Many of the men had no family and some were orphans who now knew no other life but the way of the sea. Grenfell helped organize the Fisher-Lads' Letter Writing Association in which families on shore agreed to write to a certain fisherman; and if he were in their home port, to welcome him to their home. This worked very well and had many unexpected results.

The Letter Writing Association also helped keep the young fishermen out of the taverns which in many ports were the only places where they were welcome. He helped build many Fishermen's Institutes where fisher-men could go when on shore.

Newfoundland was Britain's oldest colony and in the 1800s it was still a separate dominion linked strongly to the mother country, Britain. Until 1949 there were no ties between Newfoundland and Canada, except perhaps geographically in the dispute with Quebec over Labrador.

In 1892 Grenfell was asked to go to Newfoundland and investigate the conditions of the Newfoundland fishermen who fished on the Grand Banks. He was to see if they needed the help of the Royal National Mission to Deep Sea Fishermen. He left England to cross the Atlantic in the middle of the summer. His vessel was called the *Albert,* and Grenfell remarked on the coincidence that she was exactly the size as the *Matthew* in which John Cabot had sailed across the Atlantic to discover the New World four hundred years before.

The romance, the adventure and the danger attracted Grenfell much more than the religious aspects of such a voyage. He hated to think of himself as a "missionary", and had few good things to say about those who did. He enjoyed the challenge and hard work, and he especially enjoyed helping those who needed and appreciated his help. In Newfoundland he was to find people who needed him more than he had ever thought possible.

The trip across the Atlantic was hampered by heavy fog and icebergs. Seventeen days after leaving England

St. John's, Newfoundland, after the fire of 1892

they sighted land just north of St. John's, the ancient capital city of Newfoundland. Even before they entered the harbour of this, one of the oldest cities in North America, they knew that something was terribly wrong. Over the hills rose columns of thick black smoke. As they entered The Narrows they could see that the city was burning down. The huge cathedrals were charred ruins. Ships at anchor were blazing in the city and could be seen clearly on the slopes down to the water.

Thousands of people were fleeing the burning city and clogging the roads to the country where they were trying to find new homes with friends or relatives. The city was a total ruin.

When it was safe to go ashore, Grenfell was amazed to see how calmly the people were taking the disaster. There was little complaining or condemning the authorities for the trouble. People were doing their best to remedy the situation. Grenfell was warmly received and even in these circumstances he was well treated. He later wrote, "None of us will ever forget their kindness, from the Governor Sir Terence O'Brian, and the Prime Minister, Sir William Whiteway, to the humblest stevedore on the wharves."

Grenfell was told that it would be impossible to conduct his mission on the Grand Banks for two reasons. First, the men fished in isolation, with each vessel working separately, unlike in the North Sea; and secondly, the fog was so thick that finding the vessels would be very difficult. Grenfell was advised to follow the great fleet of fishing schooners that had just gone north to the Labrador cod fishery for the summer. This he decided to do, and in the first week of August, 1892, he left St. John's and sailed north for the Labrador coast. The Newfoundland government was delighted that he was interested in helping the fishermen, and sent along a pilot and the Superintendent of Fisheries to help the doctor with his work.

Grenfell's first sight of the Labrador coast is recorded in many books that have been since written about him and his work there. He wrote:

The exhilarating memory of that day is one that will die only when we do. A glorious sun shone over an oily sea of cerulean blue, over a hundred towering icebergs of every fantastic shape, and flashing all of the colours of the rainbow from their gleaming pinnacles as they rolled in the long and lazy swell. Birds familiar and strange left the dense shoals of rippling fish, over which great flocks were hovering and quarrelling in noisy enjoyment, to wave us welcome as they swept in joyous circles overhead.

He could see in the distance the dark cliff rising thousands of vertical feet straight out of the Atlantic and edged at the bottom by a white line of foaming breakers. From these cliffs flew thousands of sea birds of every size and description. In the waters swam shoals of all kinds of fish, which have been the marvel of every explorer.

Who were the early explorers of this part of Canada?

There were schools of whales that swam up to the surface and at times leaped completely out of the water into the sunlight. Inland over the tops of the cliffs he could see many distant ranges of hills where no man ever walked, and the sight chilled Grenfell with delight. He was an adventurer at heart and he was filled with excitement at these rugged natural wonders.

They caught up with the Newfoundland fishing fleet at a place called Domino Run where all the vessels were at anchor. The new doctor in his mission vessel created a great deal of excitement. Everyone was anxious to learn what he was up to and delighted when they heard. There were a number of cases which required immediate attention and one of them moved Grenfell very deeply.

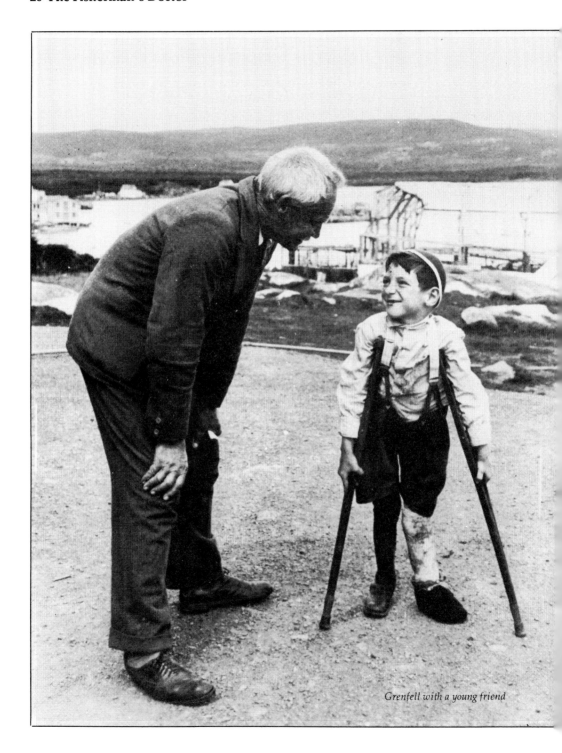

Grenfell with a young friend

A poorly dressed young boy rowed out to the doctor's boat from shore and asked if there was really a doctor aboard. Grenfell said that he was a doctor and the youngster replied, ''Us hasn't got no money, but there's a sick man ashore, if you'll come and see him?''

He led the doctor to a tiny sod-covered hovel which shocked Grenfell with its poverty and filth:

The floor was pebbles from the beach, the earth walls were damp and chilly. There were half a dozen rude bunks built in tiers around the single room, and a group of some six neglected children, frightened by our arrival, were huddled together in one corner. A very sick man was coughing his soul out in a lower bunk, while a pitiably covered woman gave him cold water to sip out of a spoon. There was no furniture except a small stove with an iron pipe leading through a hole in the roof.

After a brief observation Grenfell could see that the man had severe pneumonia, a high fever and probably tuberculosis. The doctor faced the dilemma of whether or not he should take the sick man aboard their vessel where at least he would have a comfortable bed and good treatment for the few days that remained to him. This would mean taking him away from his family and, in all probability, never bringing him back. The only chance the man had for recovery was in a hospital with a trained nursing staff. Neither even existed along the coast.

When the people of Labrador discovered Grenfell's kindness and his medical skill, they developed a great deal of trust in him.

Dr. Little, Grenfell, and one of
their patients

Frustrated, Grenfell realized his own helplessness in the face of so great a need for help. He did not falter, but in the manner of his teacher, Sir Frederick Treves, he did what he could for the dying man. He left medicine for him, food for the family and advice for the woman as to how to treat her husband. Then he prayed with the family for a time and continued on his way. When he again passed through Domino Run on his way south in the fall, the snow was already on the ground and the man was dead and buried. The widow was forced to live on a government allowance of twenty dollars a year.

In his first trip along the coast of Labrador, Grenfell found most people to be poor, and many to be unhealthy. A simple broken bone often developed into a permanent deformity because there was no one to set it properly. An abscessed tooth was a source of torture for months, and sometimes a serious infection developed. Cuts became infected and turned to gangrene. Simple ailments like ingrown toenails incapacitated people for years. Because of the dangerous nature of their work, the men often suffered from accidental wounds from guns and knives. Poor diet along the coast meant that many people suffered from scurvy, rickets, and tuberculosis, especially among the families who lived there all year round.

Because of the isolation there were few parsons along the coast. Some of the fishermen who lived on the Labrador coast often asked Grenfell if he would perform wedding ceremonies. He always declined unless he had a minister on board his vessel.

The Newfoundland government was enthusiastic about anything that could be done for the fishermen, especially because it would cost them nothing. The newspapers, Board of Trade, politicians and the governor were unanimous in praising Grenfell's efforts and pledged to help him in the future. It was with the future in mind that Grenfell set sail for England that fall. With his own eyes he had seen the problems these people faced. In his mind's eye he could see the solutions, or at least some of them, if only he could get the go-ahead from his mission headquarters. He had seen the difficulties and accepted the challenge. Grenfell was "on the case" and woe to those who stood in his way.

On the Labrador CHAPTER 5

Back home in England during the winter of 1892-3, Grenfell planned frantically for his next season of work on the Labrador coasts. He wanted a fresh load of supplies, clothing and reading materials. He wanted a steam powered vessel to serve the coasts so he wouldn't need to rely on the wind for propulsion. He had plans for the construction of two hospitals, and he hoped to enlist the aid of a number of doctors and nurses to staff them.

The National Mission to Deep Sea Fishermen, however, had some reservations about the exploits of their young superintendent. They felt that he was overstepping his authority, and also that he was ignoring the day to day work of the mission outside Labrador. This was probably all quite true. They soon issued a number of directives to "put him in his place". Grenfell was informed that in future he was "to make no appointments or changes without the direct authority of the Council. . ." Later he was informed that the mission would no longer be responsible for any cheques that he issued in their name. He was also informed that most of the money he had hoped for would not be forthcoming, at least not from the mission.

What was the evidence that the criticisms of the National Mission to Deep Sea Fishermen were justified?

Grenfell was not in the least deterred by these major setbacks. He persuaded the captain of his vessel, the *Albert*, to accompany him on a tour of England to raise the necessary money. The tour was a success.

The young missionary appeared on many platforms where he told of the horrors of life on the Labrador. He vividly told of the hunger, privation, filth, disease and especially the exploitation by the merchants and liquor traders. Everything he said was true, and Grenfell did not spare his listeners the whole sordid truth. Contributions poured in, and by spring he had enough funds for his two hospitals and a steam vessel which they named the *Princess May*.

Grenfell arrived in St. John's on June 26, 1893. Ever conscious of his parallel with John Cabot, he contrived to leave England from Cabot's home port of Bristol. On the way across the Atlantic he organized the passengers

Battle Island and Battle Harbour

The general store is in the centre of the photo. Jutting out behind the store is one of Dr. Grenfell's hospitals.

into teams for cricket on the deck. Their only problem was that the balls kept bouncing over the side. As the last cricket ball went over the side, to everybody's astonishment Grenfell leaped after it into the cold waters of the Atlantic. When the ship tacked around to look for him they found a beaming Grenfell with the cricket ball held proudly aloft for all to see.

An ocean liner brought across the *Princess May*, a thirteen-metre steam driven launch, as well as two nurses who had volunteered to staff his hospitals.

On July 6 he left St. John's in the *Princess May*, bound for Battle Harbour on the Labrador coast. The two nurses and a Dr. Curwen, who had also volunteered, set out in their sailing vessel, the *Albert*. When they arrived at Battle Harbour they inspected the building which had been donated for their use. It was a large, two-storey, wooden structure which overlooked the traders' warehouses. They immediately began stocking it with beds and supplies.

This hospital at Battle Harbour was the first one built on the Labrador coast. It was ideally situated to serve both the "Liveyeres" who stayed on the coast all year round, and the fishermen who passed it on their way to and from the seasonal Labrador fishery.

From Battle Harbour, Grenfell went on to Indian Harbour. Here he established the second hospital on the coast, and with the help of his team of volunteers he soon had them serving their needy patients. Grenfell himself did not spend much time in either of these hospitals. He used his steam launch to cruise along the coast to visit small isolated communities that were almost inaccessible to the outside world. One such visit by Dr. Grenfell is described by Mr. John Sidey, who was at this time a missionary stationed in Belle Isle Strait:

A strange-looking vessel was slowly making her way round the point. Two flags were flying, and, as she dropped anchor, we were able to read the insignia of the Mission plainly. . . We decided to go on board. Boats filled with fishermen were already on the way out. We were just ready for a start when a sharp knock came on the door and on opening it we were greeted with, "I am George Stoney, and this is Dr. Grenfell." Not much time did the worthy doctor give us for a fraternal chat. He was soon asking us about the sick and the needy, and, with a promptness that was calculated to teach us a lesson, the three of us were out visiting the poorest of the families.

One day Grenfell visited a poor family whom he had met the previous year when he treated one of their children. He had then realized how poor they were and had given the family a number of warm blankets. Darkness fell, and Grenfell was forced to stay with the family overnight, not an uncommon occurrence. A number of the children huddled together in one bed while the parents and an infant slept in another. The doctor himself slept on the floor. Cold air was coming in through cracks around the door and there was not a blanket in the house.

"Surely I left blankets with you last year?" he asked the woman in the morning.

"Yes, doctor, but I had to cut them up and sew them into clothes, for the children had not a stitch to put on."

Sure enough, the children were proudly wearing the blankets which he had brought to the house the previous summer.

Another time a big fisherman rowed over to the doctor's boat. When he climbed over the railing he put one hand to his jaw and walked over to Grenfell.

"Doctor," he said. "I wants you to treat me for a bad tooth."

"Come in and we'll have a look at it," Grenfell said.

The tooth was abscessed and badly needed removal. "It will have to come out," the doctor said.

"Come out?" the man was shocked. "No, doctor. I just wants you to charm'en, not take'en out."

At first Grenfell did not understand, but finally he did and gave the fisherman his own way. He put his finger on the offending tooth and mumbled a few senseless words and then nodded to the fisherman.

"How does that feel?" he asked doubtfully.

Battle Island is the legendary scene of early fighting between the native Inuit and Indians. It has also been called the concert platform for the loudest husky dog chorus in the world.

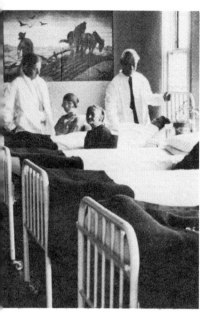

*St. Anthony Hospital
Dr. Little and Grenfell are
standing at the far end.*

"Oh, grand," was the reply. "The pain is gone out of'en all together." The contented fisherman then climbed back over the side into his own boat and rowed away.

In place of science and medicine the people had evolved curious superstitions to protect them from illness and misfortune. The fin-bone of a haddock worn around the neck was thought to be a protection against rheumatism. The head of a wolf suspended on a cord was supposed to tell which way the wind would blow by turning in the same direction. Babies suffering from eye diseases such as ophthalmia were often treated by having sugar blown into their eyes. In many cases the supposed cures were worse than the original disease.

One day Grenfell had to treat a fisherman who had suffered a hunting accident. His gun had discharged while his hand was over the muzzle. The shot had penetrated his right hand and smashed it to a bloody pulp. The man had stopped the blood by plunging the injured arm into a flour barrel and then he tied a bag around the mess of clotting blood, flesh and flour. By the time Grenfell saw the man his arm was gangrened up to the elbow and he told the man that amputation was necessary.

"No sir, I can't lose me right arm!" the man protested. "I can't fish with no arm and me family will all go hungry. Just as well die as lose me arm."

So Grenfell and his colleague were forced to treat the fellow with their best medical know-how without an amputation. His strong constitution no doubt saved the fisherman's life, for after a brief period of illness and high fever he began to recover. Grenfell performed surgery on the man's hand and fashioned a kind of hook with the smashed bone so that the fisherman could operate a boat and haul a trap. When skin was needed Grenfell and his assistant donated skin for grafts to the man's hand. Grenfell joked to the other doctor that the fisherman had Scotch Presbyterian flesh on one side of his hand and Church of England on the other side, while the rest of him was still Roman Catholic.

On his second trip to Labrador, Grenfell made contact with the Moravian missionaries from Germany who had established five mission stations on the coast. Grenfell found them very kind and self-sacrificing, but

he mused that they had never brought a doctor with
them in all their 130 years of missionary work. Their
emphasis was on saving the soul of the "heathen"
Inuit. The Moravians translated the Bible into the native
language and instructed them in the teachings of
Christianity.

    Much of the coast had not been charted, and Grenfell
soon made himself an expert with a sextant and a
compass. He drew charts and maps of the shores he
covered, and charted safe passages through the treacherous inlets and tickles. He continued this practice all
through the years he travelled the coast, and in 1911 he
was awarded the Murchison Prize from the Royal
Geographical Society for his work in charting the coast
of Labrador.

    From time to time Grenfell went farther afield and
explored some channel or passage simply for the sake of
charting, or out of his own curiosity. The awesome
beauties of Labrador have been recorded by many
explorers and navigators before and after Grenfell. The
young doctor went up many of the mysterious inlets that
run for miles inland from the coast. Hamilton Inlet was
one of them. It runs west from the coast past Rigolet, to
North West River — over 160 kilometres. Grenfell was
thrilled and amazed at the vertical cliffs rising up on

*Grenfell with the Moravian
missionaries*

*Before the arrival
of the Moravian missionaries,
the Inuit language had
never been written. The
Moravians created the symbols
for the syllabic language, which
is used to this day by the Inuit in
the eastern part of Canada.*

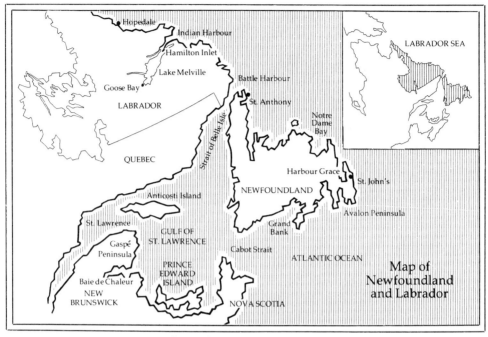

Map of Newfoundland and Labrador

either side, and the thick groves of spruce. The game was
plentiful and unaccustomed to the intrusions of man,
and the rivers were full of salmon and freshwater trout.
During this summer Grenfell's love affair with Labrador
ripened and grew.

He persuaded his crew to go into Hamilton Inlet as
far as Rigolet where the trees and plant life prospered,
out of the reach of the chilling sea winds. Here he visited
the Hudson Bay Company post and went for a picnic
with the manager and his family. He treated some of the
people, including some Inuit from the north, then he
continued his journey north to Hopedale.

And so he spent that glorious summer of 1893 and
did not notice it changing into fall. But changing it was
and the weather and the very coast itself were changing
with it. The winds were beginning to carry the chill that
hinted at worse days to come. The fishing fleets were
finishing up their work and moving south before the
annual freeze-up. As usual, Grenfell waited until the last
minute and ran into some treacherous weather on the
way south to Newfoundland. Captain Trezisse in the
Albert made St. John's; but no one heard from Grenfell
and his launch, *The Princess May*. They were reported

missing, and the governor issued a written notice to start
a search for the missing doctor. The mail steamer
carrying this order met Grenfell in Notre Dame Bay. His
compass had been swept overboard in a storm and he
was trying to steer south by following the coastline.

One of his biographers, Mr. J. Lennox Kerr, describes
Grenfell's triumphant entry into St. John's harbour in
the fall of 1893:

Despite the *Princess May's* now badly leaking boiler tubes and a
propeller shaft bent during one of her several groundings — Grenfell
called for a full head of steam and raced three steamers triumphantly
into the harbour, ending what is probably one of the most impudent
voyages ever made. Grenfell had steamed and steered this frail ex-
river craft over 3000 miles, (4800 kilometres) along one of the most
hazardous coasts in the world, a coast with no lights to help the
mariner and poorly surveyed where it had been surveyed at all. With
comparatively little experience he had found his way into dozens of
lonely settlements and explored channels where only a few fishermen,
if anyone, had penetrated before. His craft had been damaged and
dented repeatedly, his engine tested far beyond what it was made for.
Wilfred Grenfell was proud of being able to call himself a Master
Mariner: he must have known himself fully one when he made the
Princess May fast alongside the *Albert* in St. John's harbour.

*Grenfell and his wife
spending a quiet time in
one of Labrador's many
beautiful inlets*

CHAPTER 6 The Difficult Years

The next four years were very difficult for Grenfell and
his mission. He decided to go on a fund-raising tour of
Newfoundland and Canada because the mission council
in London was not supporting him with as much money
as he wanted.

He began his tour in the fall of 1893. The most
famous sealing captain, Captain Samuel Blanford, went
with Grenfell. They held meetings in St. John's, Harbour
Grace and Carbonear. From there they went to the
mainland of Canada.

Their first meeting on the mainland was at the
Orpheus Hall in Halifax. Grenfell had prepared his
speech with great care, but very few people attended. He
began his speech to a half-empty hall. His voice
quivered, he stammered, until finally, he threw aside his
speech and began to speak to the audience from his
heart.

He told them in his own words of the poverty,
disease and difficulties of the fishermen, Liveyeres and
Inuit. He described the life of people on the coast, and
ended by telling the audience about his effort to help. He
asked for their support.

The audience immediately responded to him and
they went away impressed. The *Halifax Herald* and the
Acadian Recorder praised Grenfell's lecture.

He held many other meetings where he repeated his
presentation in an informal style, and everywhere he
moved people deeply. He spoke with passion about the
needs of the people he served. He told stories from his
own experiences and the response was always positive.

His mission continued to prosper, and by 1894 his
medical team had treated 2493 patients, and performed
28 major operations and 269 minor ones. Most of these
were performed at the Battle Harbour hospital or on
board the *Albert*. Funds were being raised by various
committees, and Sir Donald Smith had offered the
money to purchase a new steamer.

But there were also many misfortunes in 1894. His

Grenfell conducting a church service on Battle Island

new steamer sank when he ran her on to a rock near Battle Harbour. The spring ice break-up was late and the fisheries were set back until late summer. The banks of Newfoundland collapsed, and many of the merchants went bankrupt. They could no longer supply the fishermen with food and provisions for the winter.

The next year the British government sent aid to Newfoundland to help reduce the losses of the previous year. However, Grenfell himself was in trouble with one of the strongest classes of people in Newfoundland — the merchants.

Grenfell had always been troubled by the way the merchants did business and sold goods to the fishermen. They rarely used cash, but had developed a system which always kept the fishermen in debt to the merchants who sold them food and supplies.

Did the idea of setting up co-ops continue beyond Grenfell's time? What is the system of buying and selling that is used now?

Usually there was only one merchant in each of the small fishing communities. So the fishermen, who were poor and uneducated had to buy at the one store. Their purchases were usually on credit, for there was little cash in circulation. The merchant wrote into his books the total amount each of the fishermen owed. At the end of the season the merchant deducted this amount when he bought the fish. Of course, the merchant set his own price on all the items sold — nets, food, hooks, twine, clothing. So the fishermen usually found themselves in debt to the merchant at the end of each season.

Some merchants were fair to the fishermen, but others were not. The fishermen were thus kept poor and dependent upon the merchant.

Grenfell could see that the merchants had all to gain by keeping the fishermen uneducated. They did not care if Grenfell healed the sick, but they objected when he tried to help the fishermen out of their poverty and ignorance. What Grenfell wanted to do was to change the economic system of the coast.

His plan was to help the fishermen set up their own stores. They would cooperate with each other and pay a manager to run their store. This store would buy their fish and sell them goods, all at fair prices.

The merchants were furious when they first heard of Grenfell's planned cooperatives. Their anger caused many poor fishermen to refuse to help Grenfell. Other fishermen feared the new plan would fail and they would have to return to the merchants.

The first community where Grenfell tried his plan was the tiny settlement of Red Bay on the Labrador coast. A young fisherman named William Pike became the first manager of the co-op. The store went on to help the fishermen remove themselves from the bondage to the merchant system.

Many other co-ops were started on the coast. Some were successful and others weren't. But wherever one succeeded, the fishermen no longer had to pay outrageous prices for their provisions. They also marketed their own fish and received fair prices.

Grenfell had created new enemies, but for the time being their opposition was not strong enough to hinder what he wanted to do.

Grenfell as a Northerner

Grenfell's CHAPTER 7
Enemies

Grenfell's mission council in England was not happy
with all the fund raising Grenfell did in Canada. They
asked him to go to the North Sea, and for the next two
and a half years he was forbidden to return to Labrador.
In Grenfell's absence, Dr. Willway was in charge of the
Labrador mission.

In the North Sea, Grenfell worked hard. He opened
meeting halls and hotels for the fishermen at ports such as
Grimsby, Aberdeen, Fleetwood, Milford Haven and others.

But his heart was in Labrador, and he planned for the
days of his return. He still spoke to large British
audiences to help publicize the mission, and he never
failed to tell them about Labrador. He recalled for his
audiences the hardships and the struggles he had
witnessed. He told of the great need, the poverty, the
ignorance, the suffering and the isolation. He made
people weep as he told them about the little Inuit boy,
Pomiuk, who had been rescued by the mission, but who
had died of his injuries while in their care. Grenfell read
letters from the boy to his audiences in England.

He began a special fund for a new hospital ship,
which would cost over three thousand pounds, for the
Labrador coast. The council objected to the several
"special" funds Grenfell was collecting for Labrador, for
they saw their regular contributors in England donating
to Grenfell's Labrador funds instead of supporting the
mission in its overall work.

At the mission council's general meeting in 1898 he
was forbidden to speak on Labrador, but Grenfell could
not be stopped. He appealed to his audience for funding
to purchase his new Labrador hospital ship. He had
already raised half the necessary sum. Dr. Willway, who
had been asked to speak on Labrador, was hesitant
about committing so much money until more funds
could be guaranteed to maintain the vessel. The ship,
Willway cautioned, would cost another thousand
pounds a year to run.

The situation was like the time when Grenfell, as a young boy, was cautioned by his brother, Al, that it made no sense to shoot sea birds without a dog to retrieve them. Willway offered the words of caution, but Grenfell did not hesitate. He trusted God, or his own resources, to supply the needs as they arose. After Grenfell's appeal, a member of the audience arose and pledged one hundred pounds of his own money if the others would do the same.

One biographer records: "The sum was raised and the keel for the new ship was laid down at the shipyard in Dartmouth. Grenfell had 'run away' with it again. His next ambition was to sail the hospital ship across the Atlantic."

In the end, several factors helped Grenfell get his own way. Dr. Willway's wife became seriously ill from the strain of living in Labrador. Willway had to leave and a new superintendent was needed. Of course, no one was more qualified or more willing than Grenfell, and his appeals for "special funds" for Labrador had become a real drain on the mission's regular British contributors. They saw this as the chance to get him out of England.

In the fall of 1899 he steamed back into Battle Harbour to a hero's welcome, almost three years since he had last been in Labrador. Flags were flown and guns

Grenfell with the huskies. Grenfell was dependent on the dogs for his transportation on land. What is the method of transportation used in the North today?

were fired by the fishermen and hospital staff. Grenfell's name had become almost legendary along the coast, although the resident doctor, Dr. Apolard was probably just as good a physician.

For the rest of the fall he served on the Labrador coast, going as far north as Rigolet. There was much to do, for in spite of the two hospitals, disease and malnutrition were rampant. There had been appeals from the people of St. Anthony, asking him to set up a hospital there on the northwestern strip of Newfoundland, called the French Shore. It was there that he docked his vessel in the fall of 1899, as the harbours began to freeze in for the winter. He spoke with the people of the settlement and with the merchant, Mr. George Moore, and agreed to service a hospital there if the people would build it. Grenfell agreed to stay all winter and help with the construction.

From photographs and records available, Grenfell seems to have taken to his first winter on the coast with relish. He learned how to drive a ten-dog team of huskies and a komatik and he dressed and lived as the people did. Once he could manage the dog team and the five-metre komatik, he undertook long trips over the snow and frozen ice to visit the sick of his scattered "practice".

Grenfell discovered that people oppressed by poverty, isolation and malnutrition have little time for fun. He found that many of the people spent absolutely none of their time in recreation and knew no games of any kind. He transformed the courthouse and jail into a club room which he furnished with books, magazines and Bible texts. He hung flags of England, the United States and the International Red Cross inside. The settlers made tables and chairs and Grenfell sent to St. John's for games of dominoes, checkers and bagatelle. He marked out a football field on the harbour ice, and taught old and young alike how to play soccer.

On Christmas Day he erected a huge Christmas tree and organized sports competitions on the ice. He held an obstacle course over a wrecked schooner and under seal nets, and organized shooting competitions. There were presents for all the children and the day ended with a concert. He was not a grim missionary who came only to "save souls". He was genuinely concerned with the quality of the lives of all the people he served.

By the time the ice cleared in the spring of 1900, Grenfell and the settlers had cut 350 trees for their new hospital. No work could begin then, as the men had to prepare for the spring fishery.

Grenfell, too, began his summer's work touring the coast. This summer the new vessel, *Strathcona*, arrived from England. She was the best equipped steamer on the coast to that date. She was thirty metres long and her hull was of steel. She had a small hospital on board consisting of six cots, a dispensary and X-ray equipment. She also had electric lights and a bathroom. Grenfell was very proud of his new boat. The words "Follow Me And I Will Make You Fishers of Men" were engraved on the steering wheel.

Towards the end of the summer he steamed back to St. Anthony, for he had been permitted to stay another winter on the coast. His name had become so closely associated with the Labrador mission that he could not be separated from it. Once again the indomitable Grenfell had his own way: from 1900 onwards, the mission office could only agree with his decisions on Labrador matters.

He stayed in St. Anthony during the following winter of 1900-1901 and it seemed as if he wanted to make up for the three years he had been absent from the coast. The hospital was soon built and staffed with mission doctors and nurses.

Grenfell also built an orphanage at St. Anthony for the children whose parents had died through hunting or fishing accidents. On his tours he arranged for clothes, games and toys to be donated to the children. He accepted children of families from all different churches, as he later accepted them into his non-denominational school.

Grenfell lamented the fact that when churches would not work together the result was that there would be two or three schools in one tiny community which could hardly support one. The schools then had to split up the government money two or three ways and the result was poor schools for everyone. Only the least qualified teachers could be afforded and the quality of education was hopeless. Grenfell condemned the churches for this denominational pride and told them of the harm it was causing on the coast.

His continued attacks angered the powerful churches in Newfoundland. They, too, liked things the way they had been before Grenfell had begun to interfere. The churches were soon to become another enemy to add to Grenfell's growing list.

The merchants, liquor traders, and church leaders were the elite — the "establishment" — who ruled over the coast. Their power came from the poor and ignorant they claimed to serve. For the remainder of his life, Grenfell was the object of attack from these established authorities.

Grenfell spent a lot of his life on boats. Here he is on the Strathcona. *He was proud of his sailing accomplishments.*

Their attacks became public when Grenfell, acting as a justice of peace, arrested a notorious liquor trader named Jewett. His enemies sent letters to the papers:

"...there is no doubt about it, he (Grenfell) has made considerable money by his mission."

The Archbishop of St. John's wrote a public letter:

If Dr. Grenfell is ever overwhelmed with a spirit of humanity...of Christian charity, could he not find ample fields for his overflowing zeal nearer home? Grenfell is not needed on that shore and his work is not only useless but worse than useless. It is demoralizing, paupering and degrading.

This most bitter attack accuses Grenfell of making beggars of the people by giving them free food, clothes and supplies. In their fury to destroy Grenfell, his enemies contradicted one another's arguments.

The Archbishop's claim is echoed even by people today. They feel that the people of Labrador were fine before Grenfell came along. True, they had their own

Grenfell had a very special feeling toward children, and according to people who knew him, the children loved him. He would sometimes stop in for tea at the orphanage at St. Anthony.

language, religion and life style, but they also had
starvation and disease. They had had a life expectancy
and infant mortality rate that would shock the most
bitter critic.

Tuberculosis, beri-beri, pneumonia, typhoid and
death from simple infections were some of the ghosts
that haunted the people. Grenfell brought healing, but
no one welcomed him except the people he served.

Another common criticism of Grenfell was that he
exaggerated the poverty and destitution which he found
in Newfoundland and Labrador. This also is probably
true. Grenfell toured the United States and England on
speaking engagements where he raised funds for his
hospitals, and the hospital ships. There was no real need
for him to exaggerate, for the reality alone would have
shocked his audiences. He was describing a world that
was as foreign to them as the far side of the moon.

*The garden at the orphanage at
St. Anthony*

CHAPTER 8 **Adrift on an Ice Pan**

On Easter Sunday, 1908, Grenfell was returning to St. Anthony hospital from church services. A man came running up to him. The fellow had come over ninety kilometres by dog team to bring the doctor to a boy suffering from a serious hip infection.

Grenfell did not wait for the man and his companions to rest their dogs and start back with him. His eight-dog team was soon far ahead of the messengers, and for a time all went well. His route took him around the edge of a harbour in Hare Bay. The ice had packed in around the land for about half a kilometre out into the bay.

As he made his way around the bay following the shore ice, he noticed an island in the middle of the bay with a solid route of ice all the way out to it. The ice continued to the other side of the bay across the island. If he could use this direct route he could save himself a great distance around the shoreline.

The ice was held against the land by an easterly wind and Grenfell reached the island easily. But when he started over the ice toward the far shore, the wind changed. The ice began to separate into pans and Grenfell's dog team and komatik were soon sinking through the soft slob ice between the pans, and into the icy waters of the North Atlantic.

Grenfell kicked off his oilskins and scrambled over the slob ice on his hands to cut the dogs' traces. The komatik was already sinking out of sight. He tied the end trace to his waist and floundered around with his dogs trying to find a pan solid enough to hold them up. He recalled,

My leading dog was wallowing about near a piece of snow, packed and frozen together like a huge snowball, some 25 yards away. Upon this he managed to scramble. He shook the ice and water from his shaggy coat and turned to look for me. Perched up there out of the frigid water he seemed to think the situation the most natural in the world.

Using the dog's trace, Grenfell managed to drag himself to the small pan and all his dogs sat around him.

Grenfell with his beloved dog Jack

Grenfell after his rescue

He is holding up the flagpole made with dog bones.

The pans continued to drift apart and soon he saw that the loose ice was drifting out to open sea.

His only chance of survival was to reach a larger pan and wait until someone came out to rescue him. Twenty metres away he saw a larger pan and began to devise a way to reach it. He cut and tied all the dogs' traces in a single line and tried to get one of them to take the line to this larger pan. None could be induced to go to the new pan with the line tied around him, even though Grenfell threw them off his smaller pan in the direction of the desired goal.

Then Grenfell noticed his small black spaniel and tied the lead trace around him. After pointing out the direction, he threw a piece of ice to the larger pan and the spaniel went out after it. The other dogs followed and Grenfell jumped into the slob ice, sliding over the top for a few moments before he fell through. Using the traces as a rope he dragged himself to the ice pan.

Once there, Grenfell sized up the situation. He was drifting not on a pan of solid ice, but on pieces of slob ice which had frozen together. He knew, as he drifted out to open sea, that soon the slob ice would break up and his pan would break apart beneath him. He was forced to kill and skin three of his dogs to make a fur coat to protect him from the wind blowing against his back. This same cutting wind moved him farther and farther out to sea.

He took off his clothes piece by piece and wrung the freezing water from them. He unravelled the ropes from his dogs' harnesses and stuffed this oakum into his boots.

As night approached he forced one of his dogs to lie down and, curling up beside him, went to sleep. He awoke around midnight to find himself shivering madly. The moon was rising over a sea that had gone suddenly calm. At least he was no longer being driven out to sea. He turned over and fell asleep once again.

At daybreak he constructed a flag pole from the frozen legs of his slain dogs and used his shirt as a flag. His matches were all wet, so he laid them out in the sun to dry. He was searching about the pan for a bit of transparent ice with which to make a magnifying glass when he saw a glimmer on the horizon. It was the flash of a wet oar. Rescue was at hand! When his rescuers got within shouting distance he heard the men yelling: "Don't get excited! Keep on the pan where you are!" Grenfell recalled later that they were more excited than he was.

Full of emotion, the men lifted him from the ice pan into their boat. They gave him a drink of hot tea and started back to shore. From records of the event, he was more than a little delirious when they reached shore. He demanded a fresh team of dogs in order to drive back to St. Anthony. The fishermen refused because of his condition and forced him to lie on a komatik for the journey. He was angry, but they would not let him go alone. His feet had frozen and pain shot through his body as circulation returned to his body.

When he arrived at St. Anthony his friends hardly recognized him. His face had turned a dark red, his eyes were bloodshot and he had aged like an old man. His fingers and hands were swollen and his voice was almost gone as he tried to recount his experience to Dr. Little and his astounded staff. He insisted that they bring his dog-leg flag pole so that he could show them how he had made it.

He wanted to sing them a hymn he had heard in his mind during his ordeal, and he became very angry when Dr. Little gave him a strong sedative. His wounds were treated — he had been bitten several times by the dogs he killed — and his swollen feet were packed with hot water bottles.

The next morning he was awake early and demanded to be allowed up. He angrily abused Dr. Little, who gave him morphine, and he determinedly went to meet the people who had travelled to St. Anthony to see him. They all wanted to tell him how glad they were that he had survived his ordeal. Four days later he was organizing a fishing expedition for fresh spring trout.

He had been lucky to survive the ice pan adventure. Although Grenfell did not realize it at the time, he had not been spotted by his friends who were following him by dog team. They had not followed him immediately but had decided to wait a day until it became easier to travel. They figured that Grenfell had done the same. He was spotted floating out of Hare Bay towards open sea by a man in one of the settlements of Hare Bay, who was looking out to sea for seals. A man floating on a pan of ice was a mere speck on the horizon and Grenfell was seen only because the fellow had a telescope — the only telescope on that shore.

Besides his luck, Grenfell's energy and endurance were well above those of an ordinary man. He prided himself on his hardy strength and physical abilities. Captain Bob Bartlett from Brigus, Newfoundland, was surprised at this on a number of occasions. He was once on a hunting trip with Grenfell and their guide, and he thought the hike would test the tenderfoot Englishman. He found to his surprise that both he and the guide were having trouble keeping up with Grenfell. When they reached a lake the guide cut a hole in the ice for some fresh water. Grenfell promptly enlarged the hole and had a bath in the icy water. He later removed Bartlett's tonsils by holding the seaman up against a shed with one

Grenfell (right) with Admiral Peary in 1906

hand and extracting the troublesome tonsils with the other. Bartlett was the pilot who brought Admiral Peary within 320 kilometres of the North Pole on his successful conquest in 1909.

Grenfell dictated his ice pan experiences to Jessie Luther and later wrote it up as *Adrift On An Ice Pan*, his best-selling book. Even today it makes very interesting reading. It added to his fame, and contributions poured in from readers all over the country. His enemies claimed that he had engineered it as a publicity stunt. One person who had read it was an attractive young woman who happened to be travelling with him on board the *Mauretania* the following year. She was surprised that he would lecture her against her life as an American socialite. She was even more surprised when he asked her to marry him.

CHAPTER 9 **Other Adventures**

Grenfell's mind was always full of ideas to improve the lives of the people along the coast. The majority of his schemes failed, but some proved successful and provided benefits for years after his death.

He pressured the government to put lights and markers along the coast, starting with Indian Tickle and Battle Harbour. He persuaded the United States to lower their postal rates to Newfoundland. He opened many successful nursing stations, such as the one at Forteau, and he built a huge fishermen's institute and home for outport girls in St. John's. He opened ten co-operative stores along the coast, he built and ran an orphanage at St. Anthony, and created a travelling library of some 3700 books which was moved about the coast by boat. He brought many games and toys to Labrador's children.

One of his most bizarre schemes was the introduction of reindeer herds from Lapland to St. Anthony. He apologetically describes the incident as "The Reindeer Experiment" in his autobiography. His plan was to keep reindeer for their meat and as draft animals (for pulling loads).

He writes, "We lost 250 deer one winter." In addition, when he moved them to a spot near another village on a high bluff, over a hundred died in the summer; either, according to the reports of the herders, from being driven over the cliffs by dogs, or of a sickness. Many were shot by the local hunters. Grenfell had even imported a group of Lapland reindeer herders with the animals. The Lapps grew tired of their new home and after the first winter went back to Lapland because of the unusual cold weather of northern Newfoundland.

Grenfell continued to experiment with various northern grains which he thought might grow along the coast. The growing season was so short that none was very successful. He tried sheep and goats, but both were destroyed by the sled dogs.

Commander Robert E. Peary in his fur suit

This was Peary's message when he reached the North Pole: "Have made good at last. Have the old Pole. I reached it on April 6th, 1909."
What other attempts were made at reaching the North Pole?

Grenfell with Anne at Battle Harbour

We must try to see Grenfell in the context of his times. The early years of this century were characterized by a spirit of invention and adventure. Peary and Amundsen were on their way to the poles; scientists were experimenting with radio communication, steam engines, the telephone and the internal combustion engine. With intelligence and technology it seemed that men and women could surmount any problem. The "unsinkable" *Titanic* was launched and lost. Grenfell was part of this age of adventure, invention, trial and error.

In 1909 Grenfell embarked upon another adventure. He decided to marry. He met his wife-to-be on the steamer *Mauretania* while on his way across the Atlantic from England in the spring of 1909. He proposed to her before he even knew her name, which tells us a lot about his character. They were married in the fall of the same year.

Her name was Anne MacClanahan and she was the daughter of a former officer in the Confederate army during the American Civil War. She was well-to-do and had grown up in the richest social circles of Chicago. She was returning from a three-year tour of Europe when she met Grenfell. He was then forty-three years old and well known, if not world famous. He was energetic, quite handsome, and looked younger than his years.

Grenfell brought her to St. Anthony in January of 1910. The mission staff and Liveyers had prepared a royal welcome for the new mistress of the mission.

Grenfell built a large house for them to live in and to serve as headquarters for his mission operations. J.L. Kerr writes of the new Mrs. Grenfell:

She was well able to handle most problems. The morning after her arrival she was borrowing an apron and directing the furnishing of her home with a cool and composed authority. She was demanding a cook and solving the problem of a leaky roof in a manner that made the Mission staff realize that a new personality had arrived. They were to find, in the months that followed, that Mrs. Grenfell was not only capable but fully conscious of being consort to one who was almost a king in this northern land, and intended to make this clear.

Anne Grenfell did not fit into the way of life in St. Anthony as well as her husband. In her new home she tried to build a world similar to the one to which she was accustomed in America. Friends of Grenfell no longer felt welcome to drop in on the doctor. Under her

Outdoor tea break

influence Grenfell became more removed from the people he served, and became more of an administrator.

She travelled with him that summer to visit his beloved coast and see the works that went on there. They sailed on the *Strathcona* and Anne did not seem to enjoy the trip as much as Grenfell had hoped. Kerr reports that she did not share the doctor's pleasure when Grenfell was presented with barrels of half rotted whale meat for his dogs,

. . .or enjoy to be shipmates with piles of dried and salted fish. Her idea of social entertainment was not sitting in a smoke-filled tilt or being entertained by somewhat odorous fishermen on board their schooners. Grenfell gave little thought to food, but he had a fondness which his wife could not share for the glutinous mess that is boiled cod's heads, and Labrador's favourite "browse", soaked ship's biscuit mixed with cod and served with crisped pork fat. Mrs. Grenfell preferred less colourful dishes and more ordered surroundings.

The regal bearing and manner she adopted were rather pompous at times. For example, when asked by a customs official if they had any liquor to declare, she replied, "My husband does not allow any strong drinks in his colonies." She insisted that Grenfell be recognized as the "founder and principal figure" in the mission. Sometimes she offended the mission staff who had worked in accord with Grenfell for years. She became his executive assitant, deciding who would see him and when. She often refused interviews to people who wanted to speak with Grenfell. She handled his correspondence and helped him to edit his books and other literary ventures. She later took over the task of raising funds, under the mission's auspices, to send children of the coast to schools in Canada and the United States.

Grenfell with his colleagues: Dr. Green, Dr. Armentrag (standing), and Dr. Little sitting beside Grenfell

Grenfell always loved her dearly. His own life on the coast had been rough and primitive. She lent his life comfort and refinement, and he enjoyed it. For her part, she did all in her power to further his work, his reputation and his happiness.

Other workers in the mission contributed as much, or more. Dr. Little earned renown for himself and for the St. Anthony hospital where he served. He was a brilliant and successful surgeon and his special study on the disease beri-beri helped eradicate it from the coast. Doctor Hare was based at the Harrington hospital and travelled the coast in both summer and winter.

Doctor Harry Padon was a young Englishman who heard Grenfell speak at Repton school and followed in the doctor's footsteps. He was in charge of the hospital at Indian Harbour. He enlarged that hospital and then built winter hospitals at Mud Lake and North West River. He married a mission nurse, and his son followed him as a Labrador missionary. By 1914 there were four hospitals and six nursing stations along the coast, and over 6000 patients were being treated every year. The mission was spending over 66 000 pounds annually, and Grenfell's speaking tours were the prime source of its income. His work on the coast was growing and bearing fruit, although much trouble and heartache lay ahead.

Dr. Curtis and Grenfell on the steps of the orphanage

Changes at the Mission CHAPTER 10

Grenfell took pride in conquering obstacles, in struggling ceaselessly guided only by his own conviction that he was right. He was proud of his physique and endurance. His philosophy was straighforward. He had no doubts about the existence of God and eternal justice, or that goodness and justice would eventually triumph in the universe.

He had come to Labrador as a wide-eyed idealist who operated with a touch of the dramatic. His speeches and lectures were needed to begin interest in a Labrador mission. But once the mission had begun and spread, it needed a different kind of approach. The mission was a large operation which needed a co-ordinator, a planner and a steady organizer. Administration was the big problem facing the mission and under Grenfell it often suffered.

For example, on his lecture tours he frequently invited people to come to St. Anthony as volunteers to work for the mission or to tour with him on the

Hospital staff at St. Anthony Dr. Little is sitting on Grenfell's right, and Anne on his left. In his later years when this photo was taken, Grenfell gave over most of the medical work to others.

On the Strathcona

Strathcona. These people would turn up at St. Anthony when Grenfell was travelling on the coast. No one at the hospital would know anything about them or what to do with them. He also had a habit of making decisions and plans for the mission without consulting his co-workers, who were closely affected by the consequences. His generosity often got the mission into trouble as well, for he gave to anyone who asked him. He once stopped in at a lonely harbour to visit a fisherman who cut wood for the *Strathcona's* boilers. The man was hungry and without decent clothes. Grenfell did what he could for the man then took off his own suit and gave it to him. He then swam back to the *Strathcona* in his underwear.

Such erratic generosity only confused the over-all planning and administration of a well-run mission. The job of missionaries was not so much to give their own clothes to one fisherman, as to provide collectively for all the fishermen along the coast.

Besides, the doctors who came to Labrador after World War I were not so much spiritual, as medical missionaries. For the most part, they performed the work of doctors and left religion to the churches. Religious instruction and preaching were no longer performed by doctors as had formerly been the case. The Moravian missionaries had been sent back to Germany during the First World War, so the Labrador mission became a medical mission.

The organization of the mission underwent a big change in 1912 when Grenfell formed the I.G.A. — International Grenfell Association — which took over the running and financing of the mission. After 1912 Grenfell could finance and run the mission as he chose.

His greatest contribution to the mission in the days after World War I was not in performing surgery in the *Strathcona* as he had been doing for years. Other surgeons could operate as well or even better than Grenfell could in the isolated coves and harbours of the coast. His main value to the mission lay in his ability as a fund raiser. Since the mission could no longer look to London for finances, money had to come from contributions. Grenfell led a strenous life on the lecture circuit. He spoke before large audiences, and under his wife's guidance his message was put to the wealthy and powerful.

Though you might not recognize him, this is Grenfell as he attempted to protect himself from the black flies. About 1914.

After 1910, Anne Grenfell became more and more influential in the administration of the Grenfell Mission. She was a part of all major decision making.

She realized many things about the mission that even Grenfell did not see. She realized his importance as a fund raiser and she sought to perfect his image. She changed the once casual Grenfell into a well-dressed gentleman. She wanted him to look like a world figure and a famous man, which indeed he was. When important visitors came to St. Anthony, Grenfell shed his shoddy tweeds for an appropriate suit.

On his lecture tours, which Anne arranged and scheduled, she took care to ensure that he looked dignified and impressive. She hired two personal

The Grenfells made friends with many famous people such as Albert Schweitzer, and Alexander Graham Bell. Here they visit with Henry and Mrs. Ford.

secretaries to accompany him, and to these gentlemen was entrusted the task of making the careless and forgetful Grenfell look the part of a famous missionary. Anne Grenfell saw the importance of her husband's image to the future of their mission, and she spared no energy to build this image.

It seems that Grenfell at times resented this change in his role. He often tired of the endless lecture routine and longed to be back in the *Strathcona* preaching the gospel and healing the sick.

By this time he was almost sixty years old and it was natural that a strenuous agenda of winter lectures should tire and weaken him. In spite of this fact, these years were the most exhausting with regard to the frequency of lectures he gave. Grenfell addressed audiences daily in the United States, Canada and Great Britain. He spoke to thousands of people who came to hear him at halls, churches, conventions and luncheons given in his honour.

In 1921 Grenfell's work as a lecturer was made even more difficult by a bitter attack by the Prime Minister of Newfoundland, Sir Richard Squires. The Prime Minister expressed the sentiments of many Newfoundlanders when he criticized Grenfell's lectures. People were embarrassed by Grenfell's portrayal of Newfoundland as being destitute and exploited by dishonest politicians and merchants.

Squires had gone to the United States to try to establish trade agreements. He found that Grenfell had been there before him, and the Americans had no confidence in the Newfoundland economy. He failed in his trade mission and he blamed Grenfell. Squires appeared at a meeting of the Grenfell Association of Newfoundland and demanded that a vote be taken to censure Grenfell. His motion was turned down by the association, but he continued his attacks upon Grenfell.

Boston, 1921
The Grenfells had three children:
Wilfred, Pascoe, and Rosamund.
In the picture, Grenfell is
holding Rosamund. He is
standing with an unidentified
friend.

Treating a patient aboard one of Grenfell's boats

Many people sprang to Grenfell's defence and once again the controversy raged in the papers.

In 1922 the old *Strathcona* sank while crossing Bonavista Bay. She had been Grenfell's floating hospital, and her loss symbolized an end to his surgery work along the coast. He continued to lecture at an even more hectic pace until the officers of the Grenfell Association feared for his health. They purchased tickets for a world cruise holiday for Grenfell and Anne, knowing that he could not resist seeing the Holy Land. Instead of a relaxing cruise, Grenfell turned it into a whirl-wind fact-finding tour covering many foreign countries. He returned home early, full of new ideas for the mission.

In 1926 he suffered his first heart attack while he was hiking in Labrador. In that same year he was in London lecturing. His audiences were so huge that they filled the London Polytechnic Hall twice a day every day for several weeks. During one lecture where he shared the platform with the American temperance preacher, Pussyfoot Johnson, their lecture was interrupted by rowdies in the back of the hall. Grenfell delighted his audience by leaping from the stage and helping to throw the troublemakers out of the door.

The heart attack set him back temporarily but he was otherwise fit and strong. Unfortunately, however, he lacked the virtue of patience which is so necessary for a convalescent.

The Final Years CHAPTER 11

In 1927 Grenfell presided over his latest achievement —
the opening of a new modern hospital at St. Anthony. Its
facilities were equal to those of any hospital on the
continent. Of course, the expense was covered by
donations generated by the Grenfell mission, or more
specifically, the Grenfell lectures. The festivity was made
even more joyous when the King's representative
announced that Grenfell had been granted a Knight-
hood. The mission was now headed by Sir Wilfred and
Lady Grenfell.

In 1929 the Great Depression struck, and fund raising
was seriously hampered by the poor economic situation
in the western world. Grenfell had to work twice as hard
for half as much funding. Many of his pet projects had to
be laid aside until better times returned. Also in 1929,
Grenfell suffered his second heart attack, probably as a
result of the increased strain of his fund raising
campaigns.

Ever thoughtful for her husband, Lady Grenfell
began preparing for their retirement, when they would
both need a quiet place to live, away from the problems
and rigours of St. Anthony. She had constructed a rural
home on the shores of Lake Champlain in Vermont. She
named it Kinloch House and Grenfell was to spend his
last days there.

In 1931 Grenfell helped with his last major project,
an attempt to chart the entire coast of Labrador. The
expedition was American, named the Forbes-Grenfell
expedition and it was one of the last services he was to
perform in Labrador. In 1932 he conducted his last
summer tour of duty along the coast. He had a serious
cerebral hemorrhage in that year but he slowly
recovered most of his faculties. He spent his time at
Kinloch House as the congenial host for many visitors.
He would sit on his lawn and look out over the waters of
the great Lake Champlain. Its waters were often rough
and wind-tossed. These days must surely have reminded
him of more stormy waters where he battered his way
along a distant coast in the old *Strathcona*. Grenfell
longed for the old adventures, the old conquests and the

Two brothers who had gone hunting for curlew on the Sands of Dee, Wilfred and Algernon

Grenfell's last visit to Labrador in 1938

old friends of the coast. Patience was a virtue Grenfell lacked, and these days were a great trial for him. His spirit was still indomitable but his body was worn out.

Between 1936 and 1938 there were times when he appeared to be almost insane. He would strike out angrily at friends and visitors for little or no reason. Lady Grenfell did her best to smooth over these occasions. He dashed off hasty letters which sometimes caused further embarrassment. Once he wrote to his old mission offices in England, donating to them the Fisherman's Institute in St. John's which belonged to the International Grenfell Association. Lady Grenfell intercepted letters to prevent difficult situations.

She was not well herself in the 1930s. Although she did not tell Grenfell, she was dying of cancer. She had a number of operations but her therapy was not successful, and she suffered great pain in her final years. She kept all these things from Sir Wilfred and loyally helped him solve many of his problems. In 1938 Lady Grenfell died. Grenfell was now very ill himself. He was crippled but refused to use a wheel chair, preferring to move around on crutches.

In July 1939 Grenfell made his last visit to his beloved Labrador. Doctor Curtis was now in charge of the St. Anthony hospital. The people gave him a beautiful welcome and he was visited by many old friends. He saw again the hills and waters he had first seen forty years before as a young missionary. When he came for the first time there was hardly any medical aid from St. Anthony to Cape Chidly. On this, his last trip, the modern hospital under Dr. Curtis' direction took in one hundred patients every time the steamer landed from the coast.

He sailed north for the last time on the steamer *Kyle* and visited Cartwright. People flocked to see him.

For Grenfell's last visit to St. Anthony, everyone on the coast came to greet him, and no wonder. Grenfell's influence lives on to this day, including four hospitals, 15 nursing stations, over thirty doctors, eight dentists, and 145 nurses. Beyond the statistics, his life's contributions are immeasurable.

Younger people who knew him only in legend came to see the famous Grenfell whose name was always on their fathers' lips. Everywhere he went along the coast he was greeted with celebrations and joy. When the time came to leave, most of the people in St. Anthony came down to say good-bye. People waved and sang Auld Lang Syne as his steamer left the harbour.

His last trip to the coast improved his health in mind and body. He even lectured again briefly in the United States. When World War II broke out he wrote to Prime Minister King and urged an all out assault on Hitler's Nazis, at a time when many leaders urged appeasement. He also told King of his dreams for Newfoundland and Labrador to join the other nine provinces of Canada.

His visions, in retrospect, do not seem to be so far-fetched after all. One of his last dreams was the development of iron ore deposits in Labrador which came to pass just fifteen years after his death.

Death finally did overtake Sir Wilfred Grenfell on October 9, 1940, at Kinloch House in Vermont. It was as peaceful as a summer's evening on the Labrador coast. He had worked hard to force his dreams into reality. There had been opposition and struggle all the years of his life. It is perhaps fitting that his death was quiet and peaceful as he went to a rest he richly deserved.

It has become fashionable in recent years to criticise Grenfell's work on the coast, or condemn his "patronizing" attitudes. Perhaps this is part of a backlash against the praise written of Grenfell. It will be left to a later and more objective generation of writers to pass the final judgement, if there is to be one, on the enigmatic Doctor Grenfell.

Grenfell at Kinloch House, Vermont

Further Reading

Grenfell, Wilfred. *Adrift on an Ice Pan.* Boston: Houghton-Mifflin, 1937.

Johnston, James. *Grenfell of Labrador.* London: S.W. Partridge, 1908.

Kerr, J. Lennox. *Wilfred Grenfell — His Life and Work.* Toronto: Ryerson Press, 1959.

Mathews, Basil Joseph. *Wilfred Grenfell, the Master-Mariner.* London: S.W. Partridge, 1931.

Pumphrey, George H. *Grenfell of Labrador.* Toronto: G.G. Harrap, 1958.

Index

Credits

CBC Collection, pages
3,4,5,7,8,11,12,16,20,21,22,26,27,29,31,
32,34,37,39,40,41,42,45,48,50,51,52,53,54,55,56,
57,58,60, 61,62,63
Tom Moore, page 18
Special thanks to Terry Filgate of the CBC

Every effort has been made to credit all sources correctly. The author and publishers will welcome any information that will allow them to correct any errors and omissions.